House of Mourning

House of Mourning

Poems by

Benjamin Shalva

© 2025 Benjamin Shalva. All rights reserved.
This material may not be reproduced in any form, published,
reprinted, recorded, performed, broadcast,
rewritten or redistributed without
the explicit permission of Benjamin Shalva.
All such actions are strictly prohibited by law.

Cover design by Shay Culligan
Cover image by Zohreh Fatemi on Unsplash
Author photo by Benjamin Shalva

ISBN: 978-1-63980-832-8

Kelsay Books
502 South 1040 East, A-119
American Fork, Utah 84003
Kelsaybooks.com

for Rick Jarow
seer, teacher, friend
may his memory be blessed

Acknowledgments

Grateful acknowledgment is made to the editors of the following in which the material listed below first appeared:

Awakenings Review: "The Cup," "Hunger," "Portrait of Dr. Gachet," "Cemetery, Late Fall"
Image: "At the Breezy Time of Day"
The Orchards Poetry Journal: "Lines for Kenyon"
Pen in Hand: "House of Mourning," "Fells Point"
The Reform Jewish Quarterly: "Morning Before," "Burning Bush"
TAB: The Journal of Poetry & Poetics: "Hang in There!"

The author would like to thank the following individuals who were so instrumental in nurturing these poems and guiding this compilation: Jamie Ferrugia, Liz Minkin-Friedman, Ben Eisman, David Keplinger, Lora Berg, Tina Morrison, JC Williams, Stacie Pierpoint, Ron Vogel, Jess Skyleson, Michael Battisto, Abby Woloff, Ray Scheindlin, Julie Tonti, Mat Tonti, Ben Toth, Laura Rubenstein, and—always—Sara.

Contents

Preface   13

I

At the Breezy Time of Day   17
Morning Before   18
Three Mothers   19
After Bad News   20
Observation   21
After the Funeral   22
Survived By   23
House of Mourning   24
Sealed Meal   25
Loralee, Sixty   26
Cemetery, Late Fall   27

II

Firstborn   31
Third Date, Jerusalem, 2002   32
The Dead Sea   33
Festival   34
Jet Lag   36
Haiku   37
Flags   38
Remembrance Day   39
Photograph, Three Jewish Partisans, Benjamin Meed, 1944   41
Yellow   42
Stolpersteine   43
The Cup   44

III

Reunion	47
Hunger	48
April Lover	49
Peanut Butter, Organic, New	50
Babel	52
Burning Bush	53
Poem	54
Leaf, Howard Hodgkin, Oil on Wood	55
Better Poems	56

IV

February 8th at 4pm	59
My Daughter	60
Portrait of Dr. Gachet	61
Hang in There!	62
Self-Help Sonata	63
Fells Point	66
King of Hearts	67
Lines for Kenyon	69

Preface

Following the burial of a loved one, mourners—in Jewish tradition—go home. They sit low to the ground for seven days, in living rooms, in dens. They eat what others bring—casseroles, kugel, deli, bagels. Meanwhile, about them, family, friends, even strangers, orbit. Mourners have a density—they are a core. Mourners wrestle with insubstantiality; yet, grounded as they are, stunned and stilled for a week, they are substantial. We—the consolers—sense them, even when out of sight, even when we've retreated to the kitchen to refill coffee urns. They are different, these mourners; and, we are made different by them, possessed by an ounce of their agony, their sobriety, even—often—their relief. The lot of us—mourners and consolers alike—bound by a house.

This by design—and actualized to varying degrees. Today, a mourner sits for a week or a day or a handful of hours. Sitting may mean weaving about, flitting from room to room, guest to guest—the mourner posed as affable host. Caterers plate the nosh. Hired help scrape the plates. Hotel conference rooms replace living rooms. Virtual gatherings replace rooms altogether. Yet, however truncated or casual, however upbeat, festooned, or digitized, the house still stands. It is the arena in which we find ourselves—our bereft address—when flesh turns to bone, bone to dust, dust—to what? Bewildered, we don't know. And so, haunted, exhausted—for days or hours, in homes, hotels, online—we sit.

This is where I work. As a rabbi, hospice chaplain, and poet, this is my house. It wasn't always. Years ago, as a student in Jerusalem, I would walk with a friend whose bride-to-be had been killed, the previous summer, by a bomb in a backpack. I don't remember saying much on these walks. What could I say? What did I know of the absurdity of murder, the enormity of love lost? I only remember that I felt calm—at home—with this friend and his grief.

My own fiancé, now wife of over twenty years, remarked that she did not know how I endured each agonized march. But it didn't feel like a feat of endurance. For me—then and now—the immediacy, the vulnerability, the honesty of grief was, and continues to be, a precious distillation. The house of mourning, when we are willing, is where we get real. For a rabbi, for a chaplain and poet, this is sacred—fertile—ground.

On the morning of the seventh day, mourners rise. They circle the block, a signal to the neighbors: no more casseroles. The normal comings and goings resume. Mourning is only mourning, after all, when it is allowed to transform. I offer these poems in this spirit. They are meant to move—down to bedrock, up and out from grief. They are sorrowful, sometimes. They are also, I hope, a rising, a stretching, a circling around the block.

I

At the Breezy Time of Day

*They heard the voice of God moving through the garden
at the breezy time of day . . .*
 —Genesis 3:8

By the look of the trembling
bittercress, I would say: God

wanders the garden. That,
or a March wind leaps

like a dog at a thousand
green shins. Let it be wind.

And to every blast, every
ecstatic slap, let me say: Here.

Here I am. Though here
is a room and now a lost

hour and every man longs
for a glimpse of his God

in the suburbs. That, or he
hides in plain sight, dug in,

like the poor pachysandra,
that some people mistake for mint.

Morning Before

for M.R.

This morning, a sliver of moon said
simply: Be careful. While the sky,
spread with a jam of sunrise, cried:
Who by water? Who by fire? You

were asleep when I visited,
wrists at your ears, folded,
elbows dancing, drawing
shapes in space. I watched you

grin, grimace, grimace again.
Tomorrow, there may
be the thinnest of slivers; still,
the sky will have its answer.

Three Mothers

with the sky today
the color of milk
three mothers make

their ascent
ninety-eight seventy-three
fifty-seven they

fly
leaving no note
only

snow

After Bad News

There was, above,
a moon,
there was a tree, and nearly
to the moon, it seemed,

a V of geese, and dogs on leashes lunged
at deer, a mother and child,
and no one,
not the geese, even, seemed

to see that what they hunted
they would never catch,
not the moon, even,
circling, circling, never set.

Observation

The thunder earth makes
when, from a shovel, rosy
with rust, it falls, changes

grave by grave; but beneath
the groom's heel, glass,
triumphantly ground, sounds

for each and all the same
note.

After the Funeral

Not his eighteenth birthday
but a day or so later, my son
gave the dogs a bath.
The big one trembled—

any break in routine, even warm
water—the little one padded about,
stirred scum with her belly,
sneezed. Night

held the cold close.
And I was tired. But wet
dogs and son, whimpers and steam
said something else, something other

than death. The little one,
of course—she had shimmied
beneath the deck, sniffing, digging,
unearthing stones, burrows, bones,

finding God knows . . .
He swaddled the big one,
tenderly dabbed at her paws.
No whining, no whining, you're fine.

One of us said this; honestly,
I can't remember who.

Survived By

I thought to write: *Annie*
lashed the air with blinks;

but I found you, fatherless
daughter, asleep in his chair,

your bottom spooned
by its cool scoop, your eyes

quiet, and I knew
not to be cute, Annie, not with you,

not with fresh earth beneath your nails.

House of Mourning

Like a mouthful of rice
our mumbled devotion

page one-eighty-seven
please rise

and in the kitchen
paid women

are scraping the plates
and we are saddened

by the loss of your mother
we are saddened

by the loss of the Ravens
your mother

she was an art lover
they tell me

and your mother
they say

she loved Chihuly glass.

Sealed Meal

*Our double-wrapped kosher meals are elegantly presented,
freshly prepared, and re-heatable in any kitchen.*
—A La Karte Catering

Warm the way
a hand is warm when squeezed,
swaddled first in foil,
then crossed—the box—
by fat bands of tape,

so that I need my knife,
my black plastic knife
with its mere suggestion
of teeth—it takes time.
Others have already

bared their puck of breast,
beans, potatoes, bearded
men like me
who sigh as we saw,
sigh as we bite, who bunch

balls of cellophane
in busy fists, balls
that unfurl, flare, all
but bloom amidst the urns
and pitchers and plated sweets.

Loralee, Sixty

The small clock
beside which she sits, erect, sweatered,
swallows somehow

the stirless hour; now,
late, the light turned tea,
body steeped, ringless

fingers fast to the lamp,
she asks: *Is it dark?* Mother,
nearby, hears nothing. Again:

Is it dark? The lamp lit, but still
she asks, asking again, asking
herself alone.

Cemetery, Late Fall

Money
may not grow
on trees, but diving
leaves, flat stabs
of paint upon
the lichen slickered stone,
betray
the dash
between the dates,
the only other growth
we know, until
all we see
is gold.

II

Firstborn

Son in the city of Bauhaus
and oranges—he strolls Highway 4,
he punches
and is punched
over a girl, he prays
on the light rail, misses his stop,

nearly.
And the sea that receives him, that bathes
and, by jellied lip, births him
anew—Friday afternoons—
darkens again and again and again the incalculable
sands that are said—one grain

anyway—to represent
this boy
I would die for.

Third Date, Jerusalem, 2002

This was for us
our season. This was for us:
big love. What did we know

of nails—they fasten, we presumed,
they bind.
In a café called Moment,

we ordered toasts. With forearms,
we steadied the woozy high
top. This was the eve.

We ate. We paid. And left
a tip for our server that would never be
spent. What did we know

of detonators, of ball
bearings. Aimless, we strolled—
like no tomorrow—away.

The Dead Sea

for hersh

I remember the boy—he would have been

eight or nine—he must have forgotten, by the end
of a held breath, where it was he swam. He must have

opened his eyes beneath, bracing
for a brief sting, the way chlorine flays

the eyes, a mild blind. But up
from silken salt, I watched the boy rise, bare

his milk teeth and clap the indifferent
cliffs of Jordan with shrieks; his mother, too,

shrieking, scolding, hauling her boy by the pit
of an arm to the beach, where—

by words and fresh water—his sight
was restored. Then, quiet

swallowed this deepest place
on earth and we returned—each

to our promised delight—to swimming,
to sunning, to smearing ourselves

with mud the color of ash.

Festival

Fresh from our desert dance, they swept
our bodies—young
bronze bodies long since shed
of Polish snow—into piles, mounds,
here an arm, a breast, lips curled
demure—we knew, in the Negev, how beautiful
we had become—lovely, prideful,
pierced—verses even tattooed
about biceps, cascading script
down damp backs. When their bullets tore

through us, there was—still—
music. Music so loud
that now, in the markets—
Judah, Benjamin—on warm evenings
drinking, bass lines remind of
bullets. Forget who you pretend
you are, Benjamin,
forget who you dream yourself, Judah,
to be—you have only this:
in sands, dance. And when again they come,

in fur caps on horseback, keffiyeh
swaddled, in cool jackboots, and when they tunnel
beneath even your freshest graves
and fly—they fly, the wind even

turned foe—you will have only this choice: die, or
die dancing. And in this ninth month,
this month of birthing, I am
filled with praise, awe,
wonder—beautiful chosen—how you choose,
ever again, to dance.

Jet Lag

Blessed are the poor in spirit
       —Jesus of Nazareth

My body, believing it
evening, my eyes,
after the dark bar, blind, I cross

to a block of shade. At the Church
of the Beatitudes, yesterday:
Blessed . . . Blessed . . . Blessed . . .

I read, but could not,
for the life of me,
find my own name.

Haiku

Spill of violet
on slopes of morning snow—
my bruised belief

Flags

By the time I see it, I am
driving beneath—red, green, white,
black—pulsing with kicks of wind
like a pregnant belly, knotted
double to the chainlink, the dread

day yet starved of color,
the sky, past overpass, past
flag, a blue we see early in October,
the month fresh, fall
fresh, globe hot with storms:

Milton…Helene…Otto…Margot…Anne Marie…
Say the storm never ends.
Picture red forever
claimed, and green by them, and black.
While blue—two stripes

of sky past boxcar slats,
six pinches of winter—will
never be enough, not for us
who by desert bloom,
not for we who dream in green.

Remembrance Day

The birds take no notice,
nor the dogs, of the date—

though one finds a rib bone
and, being a day for bones, kneads

her teeth down its bleached slope—
an Adam with Eve, cleaved. You

took it from him, after all,
in a dream and so hungry

for bone, he hunted. Yes,
I hold You solely

responsible: for bone, for birdsong,
for hobnail boots.

Three Jewish Partisans in Wyszkow forest near Warsaw. United States Holocaust Memorial Museum Photo Archives #85803. Courtesy of Benjamin (Miedzyrzecki) Meed. Copyright of United States Holocaust Memorial Museum.

Photograph, Three Jewish Partisans, Benjamin Meed, 1944

for Isak Danon

they pause for you, Benjamin—
for you, they pose in snow; so fresh,
almost flirtatious, the middle one bracing
his arms as if fixing to hike the lip of his coat
and curtsy—look, Benjamin—like a lover,
the tall one blows smoke
and the sky is a seam of frayed space, a split
in a fat man's pants; Poland—

you have got to be drowned
in beautiful Jews
have you had your fill—with fists
in his pockets the last one—look
closely—he is swallowed
by faces, by flames

Yellow

Who sews a sun on his enemy's arm,
who pins his foe with a star?
Better burgundy, the color
of clay, of shed menses,
better black with gold thread
(the Romanian way),

a bug belly-up
in a cup of wine, a star
stuck in tar, a trap, better that
than this cheap, childish
felt the color of yolk, of campfire sparks,
this shard of a sun

god flying faster than gas,
seeking leaf, brittle twig, any bush
yet spent, gilding ghetto nights
bright as a Bedouin's dune,
braising sleeve and lapel
with a six-wicked flame.

Stolpersteine

Stolpersteine: brass plates, cast in concrete blocks, installed in front of the homes where victims of Nazi persecution last lived voluntarily.

Our city might have cried
but we were busy

digging.
Monuments take time.

And what is not bombed holds
its breath—no—

not a held back
scream, not Berlin,

not our city of gold
graves, baby stones

stumbling—one
to a name: Georg Krayn—

polished by the soles
of sensible shoes each

and every time
we look the wrong way.

The Cup

The cup each morning that I kiss
its belly glazed
with marching fish
a midnight blue
the fish
the lip
the handle
of the cup I kiss.

How do I know
they're marching fish
I hear no beat
fish have no feet
a single solemn line alone
may sink
or swim
or surf the Rhône.

I know
they march
because I turned the bottom up
and there was burned
the maker's mark
the killer's script
in Poland Made
the cup I kiss.

III

Reunion

On the table, tall beers
mingle, yellow, amber; bowls
of iceberg lettuce

undressed; pauses in banter
like spilled peppercorns,
and the hush of the grown,

of the old, us,
refraining, refusing to say
what it is we've been

set here to say; instead,
more beer, seared
tuna, wild rice.

Hunger

My hunger
for you is an ocean
sometimes, other times
a tantrum. I wait

for the weather
to settle, like the cloud
that swallowed the Israelites:
wretched, sun-peeled, saved. In Miami,

today, it is overcast. I walk
to the sea, dip my toes
in fury and froth, asking:
Will today be the day we split?

April Lover

There is not much left in August.
The leaves wave and say grace.
A breeze captures my hat.
I follow tumbling, trees tumbling, beetles,
shavings of lightning strikes, deer-padded grass.
We made love there—do you remember?
We had no blanket.
You pulled a tick from the track-mark
flesh at your waist.
We made love, rising, up, up,
mounting each other like ants,
following a spit scent,
knowing to hold to a shoulder, a breast,
to arch higher—
the winner, your knees pink,
your scalp burned,
the part in your hair like a binding,
a seam,
the hair of your mother, your mother's mother,
my April lover,
what wouldn't I do?

Peanut Butter, Organic, New

I take more
care with you
than with my
wife. She's alright.

She doesn't spend
the night dividing.
We won't wake
slick, anointed, soiled.

You, I have
to stab—always—
a snake escapes,
staining your label

while it dives.
Why hate your clay?
Why hate the crush
of time? But you,

you'd rather tongue
the unattained, the Formica,
than wait behaved.
And you, you'd sooner

slip beneath my ring,
oiling skin
that never sees
the sun.

Babel

The tower was never tall:
a single flight of stairs,
a door,
two rooms,
one bright with sun.

I see you there
the morning long. I think:
you would be happy
teaching poetry. I think:
how bleak

the making of a name;
though, in your case,
no act of God,
nor hand of man,
need swat your words

away,
nor smear your ink,
for you are one
alone,
one tongue.

Burning Bush

His rejection letter was kind.
It did not say
what it might have said:
that not a word was perfect. Sulking

a bit, I drove to my usual spot
and sought inspiration in bitter
coffee and a potted plant—
some shrub

tucked in a corner and stabbing
at the drywall with tongues
of green heat, craving, needle-tipped,
a terrible trying thing. I wrote

nothing worth saving that morning.
I drove home, prepared to quit.
Then I remembered
what we say of Moses:

there will never be another.
But—and here I picked up
my pen—about the burning bush,
we say no such thing.

Poem

Stop wanting
to write it,
to hack at the sadness

with oily ink. Today,
it is raining; the wind
has carried your words

to a land of fat grass,
thick as tongues, sun-drunk
berries, bees. There, they chirp

like crickets, your words,
like tiny psalms
of shameless sound.

Leaf, Howard Hodgkin, Oil on Wood

There's nothing more embarrassing than being a poet, really.
—Elizabeth Bishop

There is
a brushstroke curling
reversing returning to lap
like a wave at the wet

of its yet spent self.
Think of it, too, the leaf,
the pleat that for years—years—Howard
pained to paint, the leaf

gone, pain gone, poet
gone, too, the lot of us
leaves, the last of us
oil on wood.

Better Poems

Better poems are written quiet,
not rushed, blood
cool enough,
not bound, but not

a howl, not poor,
but watching
the mail carrier, the white car
poorly parked, loving you

the light way, letting
your ladder
be for angels, climbing,
instead, the stoop.

IV

February 8th at 4pm

Blind lids bow
before the god
of light—you believe
I've fallen asleep.

My Daughter

After we had—you and I—
shoveled some, you lay yourself
down on a spot more or less
untroubled; at sixteen, limbs

held stiff, you made no angel
in that rind of quiet cold, but closed
your eyes and I, nearby,
my job—I think—was to let be,

to keep. *You alright?* I asked.
The snow had stopped, see,
and wind checked us with slaps
of fine ice and in dark branches

above—songs gone.
You smiled, but did not answer;
finding your feet, then, we scattered
the last of the salt.

Portrait of Dr. Gachet

> *The doctor is sicker than I am, I think . . .*
> —Vincent van Gogh, in a letter to his brother
>   two weeks before his death

Eyes slim chips of sky
stained by a later hour,
later than the brush-stroked day

just past your cap—as if
the eyes, impatient
with the watched pot

of a tepid mind and blushing
blood, lunged to dusk—
these the painter paints,

seeing what we assume
you see: a madman mocking,
mocking from behind

his lime green, black
and blue; leaving you,
the doctor, nobly dethroned,

with foxglove—pretty
poison—pouring
from your humble cup.

Hang in There!

In the half bath, after therapy,
where I splash water on my face
there is a framed quotation
reminding me
that, though I am the same

age as Fitzgerald
when he drank himself to death,
nevertheless, Fitzgerald said:
For what it's worth, begin again.
Be who you want to be.

It's like that cat, I think, the one
on every guidance counselor's door,
the dangling one beneath the caption:
Hang in there!
The cat

would have to fall.
Fitzgerald too.
It's in the fling
the thing that brings us low.
But more than gravity and gin,

the biggest drag is the false
hope, the quote Fitzgerald never said,
the caption for a silent cat
who, letting go—be brave, I know—
would live to leap again.

Self-Help Sonata

I

I organized my life
this morning: what a waste
of precious time, a fortune spent

without you, dancing girl;
for all I got for all
my want was wanting; meanwhile, bells

about your ankles—*listen!*—
how they ring—*so sweet!*—
even your leaving sings . . .

II

After one
more punch,

will you
get up,

will you
be curious

about the cold?
I ask

because you happen
to have landed

in a pool of light.
Who knew!

The moon
looks good on you.

III

I wake most days and think: I didn't
win. Outside,
a girl with knobby knees

tickles the belly
of a dog. The sun bakes stars
in the paint of parked cars. Now,

what it was
I would have won,
I really couldn't say . . .

Fells Point

The song on the radio
wants to be
a different song
by maybe someone else.

The table too has thoughts
on where it has been
placed—it is screaming
and stomping its uneven feet.

And no one sees
that even the harbor has designs—
that the great glass of the hotel,
when the sun hits it right, reflects

to the billion—billion—gallons
of brackish Chesapeake
that—yes—it might
have really been someone—
might have done something wonderful—
had only it played its cards right.

King of Hearts

When my father would happen
upon a heart—this was years ago—
a stone heart, a crude valentine
carved of slim red rock
and tucked in the nook of a juniper branch, or a cypress,
or the spines of a prickly pear, my father

would seize the heart,
turn it on its side and send it skipping.
The sculptor was a man, he told me,
a guy he knew, a nice guy in town,
but the heart violated
forest service regulations—*like litter,* he said—

again, this was years ago.
We grow old.
I sit by Oak Creek and listen
for some sort of voice and hear
only water. My father
is working hard on his will, he told me—

he will send me a copy soon.
We hiked yesterday beneath a blue so blue
it seemed to be heavy with paint, to tilt, like a cheek
waiting to be kissed.
We happened upon a heart—
six of them—balanced like ornaments

in the branches of a leafless tree. My son
was with us, my wife, too—we watched
as my father sized up the tree, heavy with hearts.
It's against regulations, he said, *but the way
he balanced them, together like that, what can I say . . .*
Then he hiked on.

Lines for Kenyon

You turned still further inward,
imperturbable as a lion-gate and lived on
   —Jane Kenyon, Lines for Akhmatova

Sad for seven months;
then, grief, *like a crow*
(your words), pelted
by headlights, shocked
by pharmaceutical scree, released.

There is nothing I can do, you wrote,
against your coming. I wake
towards evening, the lot empty,
the air, past
the windshield, blue

and still. You're turned
to look at the camera, gazing
out from the cover, out past
my thumbs, your eyes like birch,
bruised, bright. You wrote:

How I love the small, swiftly
beating heart . . . the old car starts. I hold
your book in one hand
and steer with the other.

About the Author

Benjamin Shalva's poetry and prose have appeared in publications including *Image, Spirituality & Health Magazine,* and *The Washington Post.* He is the author of two books of nonfiction, *Spiritual Cross-Training* and *Ambition Addiction* (Grand Harbor Press). A rabbi and hospice chaplain, he lives in Baltimore with his wife, Sara, their two children, and their two hound dogs.

To learn more, visit:
www.benjaminshalva.com

www.ingramcontent.com/pod-product-compliance
Lightning Source LLC
Chambersburg PA
CBHW030913170426
43193CB00009BA/835